Short Stories:

I Declare Your Wondrous Work

By: Marina Sh.

Trilogy Christian Publishers

A Wholly Owned Subsidiary of Trinity Broadcasting Network

2442 MicHelle Drive

Tustin, CA 92780

Copyright © 2024 by Marina Sh.

All Scripture quotations, unless otherwise noted, taken from THE HOLY BIBLE, NEW INTERNATIONAL VERSION®, NIV® Copyright © 1973, 1978, 1984, 2011 by Biblica, Inc.® Used by permission. All rights reserved worldwide.

Scripture quotations marked (KJV) taken from The Holy Bible, King James Version. Cambridge Edition: 1769.

All rights reserved, including the right to reproduce this book or portions thereof in any form whatsoever.

For information, address Trilogy Christian Publishing

Rights Department, 2442 MicHelle Drive, Tustin, CA 92780.

Trilogy Christian Publishing/ TBN and colophon are trademarks of Trinity Broadcasting Network.

For information about special discounts for bulk purchases, please contact Trilogy Christian Publishing.

Trilogy Disclaimer: The views and content expressed in this book are those of the author and may not necessarily reflect the views and doctrine of Trilogy Christian Publishing or the Trinity Broadcasting Network.

10 9 8 7 6 5 4 3 2 1

Library of Congress Cataloging-in-Publication Data is available.

ISBN 979-8-89041-844-9

ISBN 979-8-89041-845-6 (ebook)

TABLE OF CONTENTS

My Father Who's Behind the Sky 5

The Weights 7

Your Will Be Done 11

My Father 23

Psalm 71:16-18 29

Let me tell you about my Father... 31

Introduction

My Father Who's Behind the Sky

He is the only One whom I depend on. He is the only One who sees me. Next to Him is where I belong. One looks to the sky, hearing the words, "My daughter, do not be afraid," making a great deal of indescribable emotions pass through my soul. The universe is devoted to You. Life shouldn't be tangled. While the world breaks down into pieces, the sky reaches out to you and drags you out of the pit. He is the almighty seated in the sky. Loving, compassionate, merciful, joyful GOD, MY invisible Father is. Growing up in a world with overly complicated rules and unrealistic expectations is too hard to deal with. Being wrong all the time, I am either too emotional or overreacting. With nobody holding you strong in the battles, and whenever I am in a muddy lake holding my last breath, I look up to the sky. Then the miracle happens. All troubles disappear. There my savior comes to the rescue, my Father, my GOD. HE goes with me to the ends of life, never cheats like men do, loves me unconditionally.

The only one who has seen through this fragile heart and complex mind. Balancing between the two grasps too much effort with never ending arguments. When I am too sad or downhearted, and when I am surrounded with too many close-minded hypocrites, there is a voice telling me to hold on. And despite all the negative emotions He embraces me with tenderness.

The Weights

When the power went out at night, gathering around and demanding a Bible story by candlelight was the best way to keep going. Listening to Bible stories as a child was enthralling, especially when told by one's mother. Loving the Lord, "Her Father," was ingrained in her heart and soul from a young age.

By the time the young girl reached the age of seventeen, everything had changed. Her family was defeated by the struggles and temptations of life. Her bond with the Lord grew stronger and stronger. The only survival technique she knew was remembering the Ten Commandments. Having a sacred relationship with Him and telling him, "Her Father," everything she was going through, listening to his voice and taking his advice. Her prayers were always heard. Her first priorities in life were to love and care for her family. All she knew was to love them, even in their most vulnerable and cruel moments. She took upon her the task of shielding them from everything, including themselves. She was not an eloquent speaker; therefore, it was difficult for her to communicate what was on her mind and in her heart. The single and most effective tool she had was prayer: it was the only way she knew how to carry out her intent. The Almighty's faithful soldier she was. Him honoring his promise to her was the kindest thing that had ever occurred to her.

That Saturday was filled with grace. The house of this young girl was flooded with a tremendous sense of warmth as the light of grace streamed in from every window and corner. Dinner was being made in the kitchen by the mother. The younger brother, who was portraying the male's role, was somewhere outside, while the sister was busy talking to one of her best friends.

On that day, the young girl was suddenly struck by a profound sense of grief and despair, and she felt the desire to go to her room and lie down on her bed.

She entered her room, shut the door, shut her eyes, and wrapped herself in a blanket. Then she sobbed uncontrollably. Not knowing what was going on with her She decided to be cautious because she had no explanation for the strange phenomenon she was experiencing. She didn't want her mother to hear her crying voice and find her in this tormented state. All she could do was pull her blanket all the way up to her mouth in a tight grip.

She was finally calm after several exhausting attempts to soothe herself.

As she closed her eyes, a gentle breeze touched her face, and she found herself in a place unlike any other she had seen. It was so beautiful and full of light, grace, and joy that it made anyone who entered it want to stay there for eternity. She scouted the area, looking everywhere until she spotted a transparent shield. A shield that served to differentiate between the two worlds. Something was pulling her toward that shield, and not knowing what it was, she decided to go check it out. With each step she took toward the shield, she encountered an overwhelming feeling of despair and sadness.

Looking back, she was drawn to the shield despite the amazing light and the graceful place she had just been in. Hearing the tormented souls scream for mercy was beyond any human's ability to bear. All over that place, there were burning flames, black rocks, and gray smoke. A place where Doom and Misery reigned supreme.

She began to cry hysterically as she looked in through the shield. They were present! Behind that shield were the only people she had ever loved. Knowing that they couldn't possibly survive the horrors of that place, she felt compelled to act. She began praying feverishly to her Father, Jesus in Heaven, not wanting to lose her balance and slip, in the hope of convincing Him to sacrifice herself for their deliverance. She would go above and beyond, knowing she could endure such a place for their sake. She would do everything she could to save them. Even swapping places.

When she opened her eyes, they were delivered from that God-forsaken place in a blink of an eye, as shocking as it seemed. "What a miracle!" she exclaimed. She got what she wanted. What a sigh of relief! She felt grateful and satisfied knowing that her "Father" had accepted her prayer. But those feelings were fleeting. She was perplexed. Those who were delivered to the other side, where there was light, turned their backs on her and joyfully walked towards it. They turned around and walked away, as if she had never existed. They left without saying goodbye or anything nice. She was speechless from shock. Her expression was one of perplexity, disappointment, and sadness.

"Father, what happened?" She inquired of Him.

"I loved them with all my heart, and they abandoned me as if I didn't exist!" She kept crying and sobbing hysterically.

"I don't regret asking you to switch their place with mine for a second, but they just left." They didn't even plead with you for my sake."

Realizing they had abandoned her after all of her efforts to save them, brought her to her knees with an indescribable sense of despair. Looking at the flames behind her and with a heavy heart, she accepted responsibility for her decision, knowing that even if she had to do it all over again, she would. She adored them and needed to accept reality. They were the weights that GOD had assigned to her, and it seemed like the only way for her to preserve the seeds that she had received from her Father who's in Heaven.

When she accepted that thought, she heard the gentlest voice; His light was overwhelming. Even though she was in a fiery place,

His light was so tender and full of love, and through the light a voice was heard.

"My daughter, when the whole world did not value my sacrifices, how could those whom you saved value yours?"

"I desire mercy, not sacrifice," understanding that she can only help those whom she loves by praying only.

She opened her eyes with a sigh of relief, realizing she was back in her bed. All her tears caused her eyes to swell like balloons.

She hugged herself and took solace in the fact that everything she had gone through had been a dream. A dream that could well become a reality to every one of us.

Your Will Be Done

Manana was her nickname. As she transitioned into adulthood, this young lady maintained the innocent and youthful radiance. Her expression remained pure, and her energy continued to overflow with exuberance. However, an emptiness resided within her heart. Despite her unwavering devotion to her family, the transformative experience she was about to go through was going to cause her to gain a new understanding. The dynamics of their relationship were about to undergo a significant shift. The saying, "They hear and do not understand; they see and do not understand," was applied to her relationship with her family. They were there for her and loved her, but they never knew her.

After a lengthy absence, her father retired and returned home to live with the family. She eagerly anticipated the opportunity to spend quality time with her father, tending to his needs and gaining a deeper understanding of who he was. The moment had finally come for her to gain more understanding of her father and fill that emptiness.

Having spent three long years with her father, the void in her life that she couldn't quite explain got deeper. An emptiness resided within her heart. She adored her father; he used to call her "Manna," which meant "the bread of life. Yet she couldn't help but feel that there was a certain void in their bond. Until one fateful day, something occurred that changed everything.

"Call 911!"

In the dead of night, a piercing scream shattered the silence. It was the mother, her voice echoing through the darkness. She rushed to her daughter's bedside and spoke in a hushed tone, "Your father is dying. Call the ambulance." She rushed to the living room, where he lay asleep, her eyes taking in every detail in slow motion.

As she stood there, frozen in time, the sound of her mother's cry pierced through the air. Her father's labored breathing mixed with the commotion of the ambulance arriving, creating a chaotic symphony that echoed in her mind. She was in complete shock, unable to move or speak as the events unfolded before her.

She sat in the living room, seeking comfort and anxiously awaiting her mother's arrival to soothe her with the long-awaited good news. Deceiving herself and convincing her mind into believing that it was just a phase, a passing moment that would soon fade away. Twenty minutes passed before her mother returned from the hospital. Despite the lack of emotion on her face, her heart raced with excitement to hear the good news.

"Your father is in the Intensive Care Unit." The mother's voice trembled as she spoke, "He is in critical condition," relaying the words of the doctors. She took a deep breath and convinced herself once more that he was going to be fine.

A week had passed, and nobody was allowed to see him. The only way of communicating was through the phone, and only for three minutes. Her father was the type of man who required a comforting presence. Whenever he fell ill, his eyes would light up in a manner reminiscent of a child seeking solace from his mother. Knowing that, she took it upon herself to comfort him. She couldn't deceive herself no more she got on her knees and prayed to God, "I pray to you, Father, in the name of Jesus Christ, your only son, to cure my father and bring him home again, Amen."

This young lady held a special place in her heart for a dear friend who had become an important part of her life. As she had strayed from her faith, she turned to him. She placed her trust in him to communicate her messages to the Lord. With a heavy heart and a mind full of frustration, she finally reached her breaking point and took a deep breath; it was time to take action and make a change. The urge to visit her father at the hospital overtook her. She sought the help of her dear friend to assist her in providing her father with some much-needed breathing exercises. It was her hope that these exercises would improve his overall health. Without hesitation, she made her way to the hospital, hoping that it wasn't too late.

The hospital was tightly secured, with all doors firmly shut and no admission granted without a prior appointment. With a desperate voice: "Why did you encourage me to come when I knew deep down it was impossible to get in?"

Her friend responded with a calm and reassuring voice: "I don't know. God wanted you to go; we will find out the reason later." Every word that had been spoken to her seemed to have gone over her head, leaving her with a sense of frustration. She walked back to her home, feeling perplexed and confused.

The following day, they received a surprise call from the hospital, informing them that it was time to finally visit him. As she accompanied her mother to meet him, her heart swelled with joy. Yet she kept a stoic expression on her face, betraying none of her emotions.

Seeing him in a state of utter confusion, unable to recall what had happened to him or how he had ended up in the hospital, broke her heart. The reasons behind his current predicament eluded him, leaving him feeling disoriented and lost.

With a soft eye, he turned to his daughter and said, "I'm doing the exercises that you instructed me yesterday."

Being confused herself, she asked, "Did I teach you the breathing exercise yesterday?"

Looking at her expectantly. "Indeed, you did," he responded.

"Was it me?" she asked once more.

Your Will Be Done

"You were right beside me," he said, "and you advised me of that." He replied with a tone of irritation, perplexed as to why she kept posing the same question over and over.

Without hesitation, she reached her friend, and she started describing the events, seeking an explanation for what had happened. "You remember that the doors of the hospital were closed yesterday, right?" she asked with a confused voice. She went on to describe how her father had seen her yesterday standing next to him and the various exercises that she had instructed him to perform.

Her friend, with a joyful tone, reminded her of the age-old adage, "God works in mysterious ways." He went on to explain that an angel had appeared to her father in the form of her and had delivered her message. Overwhelmed by her experience, she made her way back home and started reading the Bible.

As each day passed, her father's condition grew increasingly worse. She stood by his bedside, feeling helpless and unsure of what to do. She sang to him the songs they shared together and the funny moments they lived together, hoping that somehow her words would bring him comfort and peace and make him hold on to his life. She spent her days there, next to her father, in the intensive care unit. In that dimly lit hospital room, with a sense of hopelessness, she read the Gospel to him and prayed.

Until one day, as she was reading, he awoke with a start, his eyes wide with fear. He looked around as if he were surrounded by dark spirits. He gazed at his daughter with a tender expression, communicating his thoughts through his eyes, attempting to convey what he perceived. She began to speak, assuring him that he need not fear any harm, for she was the daughter of God. She comforted him by assuring him of her undying love.

As soon as she spoke these words, he turned his head towards her and, in a hushed tone, asked, "Why?"

"Why do I love you?" she asked. As he nodded, tears threatened to spill down her cheeks, and she struggled to compose herself before speaking. "I love you," she said, her voice quivering with emotion, "because you are my father. I have no one else in this world but you, and you have no one else but me." As soon as those words reached his ears, tears welled up in his eyes, and she was overcome with a fit of hysterical weeping.

As she made her way home, she felt a heavy weight on her chest. The events of that day had taken their toll on her, and she couldn't hold back her emotions any longer. Without hesitation, she reached out to her dear friend and let the tears flow freely. Her desperate pleas resonated through the streets, the sound of her anguished cries piercing the stillness of the night. She was determined to convey her urgent message and make the heavens hear her plea. Her heart was heavy with the weight of her request—she needed two months from God to help her father ascend to Heaven. As she spoke of the events that had transpired and the malevolent spirits that her father had encountered, a sense of dread began to consume her. It was as if her very being was gripped by the fear that her father was doomed for eternal damnation.

The veil had been lifted, and she finally understood the true meaning of Heaven and Hell. Her friend was renowned for his unbreakable spirit. No matter the situation, he never succumbed to tears. He had endured many trials and tribulations in his life, but never before had he encountered a predicament so overwhelming that it brought him to tears. He attempted to console her and explain the significance of the phrase "Your will be done," but his efforts proved futile. She was resolute in her determination to plead with God for her father's sake, despite not knowing the proper way to do so. She longed for him to have more time to prepare for his entrance into Heaven. Desperation consumed her as she pleaded for prayer from anyone who would listen, even from young children.

After one and a half months in the hospital, news had spread among those she knew that her father's condition was worse. The doctors were perplexed and unable to comprehend the situation.

They expressed their confusion, stating, "He should have passed away within the initial week of his admission to the hospital."

Listening to their words, she extended her hand towards her friend once again, urging him to seek guidance from God regarding his decision. As he observed her in a state of despair, he ultimately accepted her request. However, a mere ten minutes later, he called back and spoke with a stern and severe tone. He urged her to stop requesting prayer from others and instead have faith. It was said that her prayers had reached the Heavens above and that all that was required was patience. "Start talking to him again; he still listens to you like he used to." The words spoken were a comfort to the troubled soul. Filled with excitement, she hurried to the hospital to read passages from the Bible to him.

As she delved further into the worn pages of the book, she was struck by a profound realization. As she continued reading the Gospel of Luke, a chapter caught her eye; it was Luke 16:19-31. It felt as though she had been slapped. She paused for a moment, closed her eyes, and took a deep breath. She felt herself being transported back in time, down memory lane. She had a vision, one that she had seen long ago. "It's true," she murmured. In a state of complete disbelief and horror, she knew deep down that her vision was a reality.

As she started her quest to reconnect with her Heavenly Father, she read the Bible with a new eye. Memories that she had buried deep within her mind began to resurface. She finally remembered her childhood and her "Heavenly Father's" unconditional love.

She remembered their pure conversations and how she used to retreat to the sanctuary of her room each night. She used to recount the events of her day to him—the people she had met, the challenges she had faced, and the triumphs she had achieved. But above all, she used to seek his guidance, his wisdom, and his unwavering support.

They had the sweetest conversations: "Did you witness what occurred today, Father? How did she treat me?" as she asked her father. "I dislike her because she has done the unforgivable."

And a voice in her heart reminded her with a gentle tone, "Do not judge, and you will not be judged; do not condemn, and you will not be condemned; forgive, and you will be forgiven."

Her eyes widened in realization. "Father," she said, her voice barely above a whisper, "I forgive her." As she settled into her bed, she lifted her voice in praise to the Almighty. With a heart full of gratitude, she thanked the Lord for the blessings of the day.

With a peaceful spirit, she closed her eyes and drifted off to sleep, knowing that she was in the loving hands of her Creator. The following day, she kept her promise to him, and the feeling of making him proud filled her with immense happiness.

He was her protector, shielding her from any danger that might come her way. Whether it was an obvious threat or one that lurked in the shadows, he was always there to keep her safe. Before making a decision, he took the time to help her understand the true meaning behind the age-old adage, "You reap what you sow." The gentleness in his tone was evident. "I am the Lord, your God," spoke the divine voice, "who goes with you wherever you go." As he spoke, his words had a peaceful effect on her. From a young age, her Heavenly Father guided her, taught her the Ten Commandments, and demonstrated how to incorporate them into her daily routine.

Immediately, she understood why there was emptiness in her heart. She had lost touch with her Heavenly Father. And that's why her friend said, "Start talking to him again; he still listens to you like he used to." As she continued reading, her mind took her back to a place that she had long forgotten.

Long ago, when she made her way home from work in the dead of night, she felt a sense of unease wash over her. Glancing over her shoulder, she noticed two young men trailing her, their intentions unclear. Fear gripped her heart as she quickened her pace, her mind racing with thoughts of danger and harm. Seeking solace and protection, she began to pray fervently to her Father, to keep her safe from harm. As she made her way back home, she couldn't help but keep praying to her Father.

The following day, a phone call from their neighbors reached her mother's ears. They inquired if she had been informed about an occurrence that took place in the neighborhood. She listened intently from behind the door, overhearing a conversation about a recent police arrest.

Apparently, two men had been taken into custody for the rape of a young woman. However, during the investigation, the men pleaded with the authorities to reveal information about a particular girl they had been targeting. Strangely enough, every time they attempted to approach her, they claimed to have seen two men dressed in white garments accompanying her. They wanted to know who the girl was. Upon hearing the incident, her heart was filled with an overwhelming sense of joy. She quickly made her way to her room, where she fell to her knees and began to offer up praises to the Lord above.

All the miracles that had occurred in her life were the work of God. Though she had deliberately pushed the memories of the miracles to the back of her mind, they now flooded her thoughts, one by one. Each memory was like a puzzle piece, fitting perfectly into the larger picture of her life. She couldn't deny the truth any longer—these miracles were real, and they had happened to her.

As she recalled her life with the Lord and his unconditional love, a wave of conflicting emotions washed over her. On the one hand, she felt blessed, as she considered herself the daughter of God. On the other hand, she couldn't help but feel a sense of shame for the way she had previously taken those moments for granted and how she lost touch with the only one who ever loved and accepted her and protected her from danger. Despite her distance from the Lord, she realized that He was always there for her, watching over her every step of the way. As she gazed out the window, a feeling of profound peace settled in her heart. She came to understand the stark contrast between her Heavenly Father's and her earthly father's love. Despite everything, her resolve to bring her earthly father back to life only grew stronger.

It had been almost three months since her father's health had taken a turn for the worse. Despite his condition, she refused to lose hope. She firmly believed that the Lord had the power to bring him back from the brink of death, even in the final moments. "Father," the young lady spoke with a hopeful tone, "I long for the world to witness your miracles. I know the miracles that you have done in my life; however, I fear that if I share these wonders with others, they will dismiss them as mere figments of my imagination. They will claim that it is all in my head. It seems that nobody is willing to accept anything." She kept praying, her eyes closed, and her hands clasped tightly together. The room was quiet except for the soft sound of her whispered words. She didn't know how long she had been praying, but she knew she couldn't stop until she felt a sense of peace. So, she continued, her mind focused on her faith and her heart open to whatever answer may come. "I want to prove to everyone that you exist," she declared with a determined look to the sky.

She poured out her heart and expressed her deepest emotions to her trusted friend. He was the only earthly person who truly comprehended every aspect of her being. As the final day drew near, her soul was once again filled with unease. Seeking solace, she turned to her trusted friend, who advised her to pray and seek guidance from the Lord by means of the holy scripture. With a heavy heart, she turned to the Heavens and pleaded, "God, please reveal to me your decision."

Seeking guidance, she reached for her Bible and flipped to the eighth chapter of Romans, where she began to read about life through the Spirit. As she read the words on the page, a wave of joy washed over her. Her heart swelled with gratitude and relief as she learned that her father would live. As she shared the contents of her reading with others, their faces twisted with sympathy. "Oh, dear child," they murmured.

She walked into an empty hospital room and got to her knees. With her head bowed and covered, she closed her eyes and began to pray. As she finished her prayer, an angry voice urged her to stop praying for the sinner. That it would be unfair for the sinner to enter Heaven. Without hesitation, she reached out to her friend.

As she recounted the events that had just transpired, he said, "Don't listen to him and pray again." As she knelt in prayer, a sudden stillness overtook her. In the quiet of her heart, a gentle voice spoke, "Consider the wondrous glory that awaited your father in Heaven." As she gave a nod, she suddenly leaped up from her place, "'Heaven! means 'Death!'" Thank you, Lord, for bringing my father back to life," she whispered with tears in her eyes and made her way to her father's room.

It was six o'clock when the nurse informed the family that he was in the process of taking his final breath. In a flurry of urgency, they hurried to his room, and she urgently summoned her friend. With fervent insistence, she demanded that he offer up a prayer. He spoke with a solemn tone, "His Will be done."

"I don't want." Gasping, "Pray!" she screamed. As tears streamed down her face, she lowered herself to the floor and gazed up at the sky. After taking a deep breath with a weeping voice, she summoned the courage to utter the magic words, "Your Will be done, Father."

The clock read 11:23 p.m. She held him tightly as he took his final breath, whispering words of comfort and urging him to move towards the light. The news of his passing was announced. The absence of his presence was palpable.

As she sat there, lost in thought, the sudden ringing of her phone jolted her back to reality. Her friend with a voice filled with curiosity and concern. "May I ask you what happened?"

With a heavy heart, she uttered the words, "He is gone."

"What do you mean? It can't be. Im calling to hear the good news. I know that; I felt it. And now, we shall come to understand the ways in which God labored. He is going to show you," he said. Not comprehending what he was saying, she left the hospital and made her way back home.

At precisely 3:33 AM, the phone rang. Startled, she answered to the sound of her sister's voice. Her sister had just awoken from a vivid dream and felt compelled to share it with her. "As I stood alongside our mother in the hospital, we watched as our father emerged from his room, adorned in white garments and a radiant smile. The sight of his joyful countenance filled us with a sense of happiness and hope. As we were waiting patiently by the elevator, he took your hand, and you both made your way to a room that was called "beloved," bidding your farewells along the way."

At the same time her mother awoke, and she began to re-count her dream too. "I went to the hospital to see your father. As I entered the room, I saw a tall person, dressed in all white, standing before your father. It was impossible to see his face. That person handed a paper to your father, requesting his signature. As your father signed his name, this person vanished into thin air."

After her mother, yet another one called, and it was her brother. In a crying voice, he praised God, claiming that he saw a dream. "I was on my knees, praying, begging God to show me if my father was in a good place. As soon as I opened my eyes, I saw a huge person with his feet on Earth and his body in the sky. I remembered Isaiah sixty-six. 'The Heavens are my thrones, and the earth is my footstool.' Then, I saw a spirit come down with father's voice saying, 'What do you want, my son?' 'I want to know if you are in a good place and if you are happy.' With an overjoyed laugh, he assured me that he was alive and with the Lord. I woke up crying with happiness."

"Our father is alive!" Excitedly, the young woman reached out to her friend to share the good news. She couldn't contain her excitement and shared the wonderful news with him. In that moment, her mind was flooded with the memory of her prayer to Jesus Christ. She recalled how he had spoken to her, saying, "Consider the wondrous glory that awaited your father in Heaven." The level of joy she experienced was immense, surpassing all expectations.

As she closed her eyes and took a deep breath, she reconnected to the wellspring of existence. The importance of having a father-figure is widely recognized. Yet, in this young girl's life, the father-figure was void. However, it was not a matter of concern. Her life was full of miracles, all thanks to her incredible Father and Jesus Christ. All the knowledge she possessed was directly from God and the Holy Spirit. Throughout her journey, they stood by her side, offering guidance and protection as her mentors. Knowing that nobody would be able to comprehend the depth of her connection, she decided to keep it a secret in her heart. The bond between them was authentic and untainted, as reflected in their heartfelt exchanges.

My Father

A body so small and delicate. Long, flowing black hair cascaded down her back, framing her face perfectly. Her eyes were round and captivating, drawing you in with their beauty. When she smiled, it was a sight to behold. Her great, wide smile was accompanied by an innocent expression that only added to her charm. She had a reputation for being timid and reserved.

The young girl cherished the company of her heavenly Father. He knew her heart and her deepest secrets. They used to have long conversations. The greater part of their conversations took place in her room.

"Do you know the Ten Commandments?" Her heavenly Father asked her one day while she was getting ready for bed.

"Well, yes, of course I know them, Father. Respect your mom and dad. It is forbidden to kill. You must not engage in adultery. You must not commit theft. You must not give false testimony. You must not covet." Seconds after she said with a knowing nod, "Ah, yes, you're not supposed to worship idols." then started counting 1-2-3-4-5-6-7 and with one loud sound she called her mother "Mom, I'm missing three commandments what are they? There are three missing, what are they?" Upon hearing the rest from her mother, she promptly replied, "Okay, goodbye and thank you." The mother stepped out of the room and gently shut the door behind her. With a smile on her face said, "I told you; I knew them." She prayed and went to bed.

The most difficult class was religion. She found herself drawn to her mother's tales of faith and the teachings of Jesus Christ, more so than the formal religious classes she attended. She had never put in as much effort into studying for a religion test as she had done this time. Fortunately, on that particular day, no one in her class had come prepared for the test except for her, it was finally her moment to shine brightly. As she sat at her desk, a sense of satisfaction washed over her. She had taken the time to prepare for today's test, and it showed off. The teacher, too, seemed to take notice of her efforts, offering a nod of approval in her direction. And so began a new lesson.

On Wednesdays, it was a tradition for her mother to invite her friends over for a gathering. They would spend the time enjoying each other's company and having some much-needed relaxation. As the group conversed, one of the women began to recount a vivid dream she had experienced. She spoke of seeing Jesus Christ himself. The moment the woman spoke the words "Jesus Christ," the young girl hurriedly made her way to the living room, eager to find out what would unfold next. She lowered herself onto the floor, her eyes widening in amazement as she hung onto every word. The woman described the details of the dream with such clarity that it was as if she had truly been transported to another realm.

The girl's heart was loaded with questions "Mother! What does Jesus look like? How do we know?"

"You sure have lots of questions, my dear." The mother said looking at her daughter.

"How can we be certain that the figure we see before us is truly Jesus and not Satan in disguise? Because I've heard somewhere that Satan has the ability to take on the appearance of Jesus or even an angel of light, should he choose to do so." As she persisted in sharing her thoughts loudly, she was left with too many unanswered questions.

During that week, when they got home from school, everyone was discussing an incident at the church. The town was overjoyed by the excellent news.

"What's going on, mom?" she asked in a curious tone.

"People are visiting the Church. They assert that the statue of Maria was emitting oil." The mother replied.

"Can we visit and look?" She asked.

"Yes, of course, my child, but only with your sister," the mother responded to the girl's query.

Despite the mere one-year age gap, her elder sister was renowned for her level of rationality. During her school days, she made it a point to keep a watchful eye on her younger sister.

That evening, they prepared themselves and made their way to the church to witness the miracle. Upon their arrival, they were met with a bustling crowd of individuals vying for a chance to approach the idol and capture its image. With petite bodies, she and her sister managed to slip through the masses and make their way to the front of the crowd.

"Where is the oil?" She murmured to her sister with her eyes fixed upon the statue.

"I have no idea; we'll wait and see," her sister whispered back.

As she gazed carefully, her heavenly Father's voice suddenly spoke to her, "Thou shalt not worship idols." She drew in a deep breath, her gaze widening as she surveyed her surroundings. As if she got new eyes. A cluster of bewildered humans caught her eye, lost and unsure.

As they made their way out, the younger sister pleaded with her older sister to leave and never come back. With a heavy heart, she made a solemn commitment to herself to never return.

It was Saturday afternoon, which meant it was time for a nap. A dream caught her into a deep sleep. She was on a stormy sea, with rough winds and a boat. She noticed Jesus standing on the boat wearing a blue outfit and carrying a red shawl. He stretched out his hand to her while still standing there and motioned for her to follow him without saying a word. She initially became excited, but then she remembered, what she had questioned in her heart, "How do I know it's Jesus?"

A sudden voice spoke to her, "He can come to you in any image, but he cannot take my light or my marks of sufferings, so be careful, daughter. Look at the hands and feet."

She then told the Jesus impersonator, "I'm not coming," as she stood there, and he slowly disappeared into the sea. She quickly ran to her mother to tell her about the dream. When she asked her mother for clarification, she told her that she didn't understand and that she should go to Jesus and apologize.

Finally, summer arrived, and the siblings started fighting like any normal family would. She cried and swore aloud in the name of God that it was not her fault before going to her room. She continued to weep until her heavenly Father warned her, "Do not take your God's name in vain."

As her mother hurried inside her room and got down on her knees and said, "You know that you should not swear in the name of the Lord." as her mother gave her a tight embrace to calm her down. Attempting to dry her own tears, she said, "I know that now, but no one believes me."

As time went by, it was finally the time to leave for Lebanon and see their relatives. At the amusement park and beach, they had wonderful times. As their vacation was coming to an end, they had made the decision to visit the holy site of Harissa. People used to go there yearly; thus, it was always packed. They proceeded up the stairs to pray before the statue. The moment she prayed in the holy name of the Father, the Son, and the Holy Spirit her heart stopped her and declared, "I am the Lord your God." She immediately recalled the church incident, and while maintaining an innocent expression on her face, she said, "I want to pray to my Father." She turned around and looking at the sky, said, "Hello Father," and then she began to pray.

As the summer was drawing to an end, it was time to return home and get ready for school. She would often retreat to her room, where she would spend hours conversing with her Father. On a particular day, they began a discussion regarding the fourth commandment.

"Mother, why do we go to church on Sundays?" she yelled as she was running to her mother.

"It's the Lord's Day," her mother said while she was doing some housework.

"Why then do the Jews worship Saturday?" she questioned in an amazed voice.

The mother turned to face her daughter and stated, "Their Ten Commandments say that they should keep Saturday."

"Why do we worship Sunday but not Saturday, then?" She added.

"Because Jesus changed it to Sunday, that's why," The mother said.

"But Jesus said, 'I did not come to abolish, but to fulfill.' How come he changed only that command?" she thought out loud.

In an annoyed voice, "I'm not sure, honey; now allow me to complete my job."

She returned to her room after not receiving a sufficient or satisfactory response.

As she approached her teenage years, the young lady made her way into a new phase of life. As time passed, her affection towards her "Father" deepened. Unlike many teenagers who crave independence and the freedom to dress as they please. She was different.

A rumor had been circulating among her friends that she was considering becoming a nun.

"I don't want to be a nun," one day she declared to her friends.

"Are you certain?" Her friend said, with a doubtful voice and with a sly laugh. "Because you are acting like one."

"I simply cannot bear the thought of how others might perceive me. I am my Father's daughter." As she spoke those words, their attention was suddenly drawn to the sound of music, causing them to tune her out.

After a long day, she finally arrived home and made her way to her room. Once there, she began to speak with her Father.

"Father," she said, her voice laced with uncertainty. "Do you know why I don't want to dress like them?" She paused, took a deep breath, with a frustrated voice she uttered the words, "No one seems to understand. I simply cannot envision myself wearing such clothing and feeling comfortable."

Upon hearing her out, her Father responded with a gentle tone, saying, "Daughter, your body is a temple of the Lord."

A deep sense of peace settled within her heart. She felt a quiet contentment that filled her with a sense of pride knowing that she was doing the right thing.

As time passed, she flourished and matured, and her unwavering belief in the existence of her Heavenly Father, the Son, Jesus Christ, and the Holy Spirit only grew stronger. Miracles seemed to follow her every step of the way. However, she was unprepared for the years that lay ahead. As the challenges and obstacles of life presented themselves, she found herself faced with difficult decisions. She had to determine where her loyalties truly lay.

PSALM 71:16-18

[16] I will go in the strength of the Lord God: I will make mention of thy righteousness, even of thine only. [17] O God, thou hast taught me from my youth: and hitherto have I declared thy wondrous works. [18] Now also when I am old and grey-headed, O God, forsake me not; until I have shewed thy strength unto this generation, and thy power to everyone that is to come.

Let me tell you about my Father

The age-old question that seems to be on everyone's lips is, "Why do bad things happen to good people?" It is a question that has been debated and discussed for centuries. However, one cannot help but wonder, "Why do bad things happen?" It seems hypocritical to question the actions of a higher power for, He who really knows what's in our hearts.

Don't bring up your God in front of me. Allow me to witness His magnificence and work in your life. Don't tell me I'm the servant of the Almighty, the Great, the Creator, and the Lover, and your life is ruined. I must see God in your life, in every detail of your life, in your needs, in your money, in your wisdom, in your success, in your work, in your victory, and in your children. I need to see God's work in your life to know that you believe in the true God.

You can't tell me that you are following the true religion and following the true prophet while your children are starving, your youth are dying, and your patients are dying, as if they had no God to heal them. Because the Lord of promises is the true God. There are promises made by the Lord God to those who believe in Him, obey His commands, memorize His Gospel, and trust in His Son.

Let me tell you about my Father and His promises for those who follow Him and accept Jesus Christ as the son of God and the Savior. Our Father's promises are numerous for his children, but I will only name a few.

In Zechariah 2:8, He spoke, "For whoever touches you touches the apple of his eye."

In John 16:24, we are told, "Until now you have not asked for anything in my name. Ask and you will receive, and your joy will be complete."

To those who proclaim, "We endure suffering in this life, and shall be rewarded with entry into Heaven," I will remind you, in the teachings of Jesus Christ, there is a connection made between sickness and sin. With each person he healed, he imparted a solemn instruction seen in John 5:14 "See, you are well! Stop sinning or something worse may happen to you."

He also said in Matthew 17:20-21, "Truly, I tell you, if you have faith as small as a mustard seed, you can say to this mountain, 'Move from here to there,' and it will move. Nothing will be impossible for you."

For when has our Father ever desired to witness the affliction of His beloved children? The kingdom, it is said, begins in this life and extends beyond our mortal existence. How do we know that? Because He who has risen from the dead told us. Matthew 19:29, the Lord Jesus Christ declares, "And everyone who has left houses or brothers or sisters or father or mother or wife or children or fields for my sake will receive a hundred times as much and will inherit eternal life."

In Isaiah 43:1, we are told, "Fear not, for I have redeemed you; I have called you by name; and you are mine." Imagine he called our names one by one, and your name is carved on his palm and recorded in the Heavens above.

In Philippians 4:13, Paul states, "I can do all things through Christ, who strengthened me." I can win; I can triumph; I can accomplish my desires; I can do everything. Why? He strengthens me because I have a Christ who has risen from the grave, who is a creator of miracles and the Lord of miracles.

No one who walks in the way of the Lord is unsuccessful. Psalm 1:3 tells us, "And he shall be like a tree planted by the rivers of water, that bringeth forth his fruit in his season; his leaf also shall not wither; and whatsoever he doeth shall prosper." How are we going to succeed? Because I serve a Lord and a God who promised me victory in whatever I do. Let's talk about pampering in Isaiah 66:12: "For this is what the Lord says: will extend peace to her like a river, and the wealth of nations like a flooding stream; you will nurse and be carried on her arm and dandled on her knees."

Vigor and perpetual youth. It is not possible to see a person with energy and permanent youth, who is not one of the missionaries of the Lord Jesus Christ. Isaiah 31:40 says, " But those who hope in the Lord will renew their strength. They will soar on wings like eagles. They will run and not grow weary. They will walk and not be faint." These are the promises of the Lord to us.

We are told about famine in Joel 2:26, "You shall eat in plenty and be satisfied, and praise the name of the LORD your God, who has dealt wondrously with you. And my people shall never again be put to shame."

On the level of understanding and wisdom, Proverbs 1:23 says, "Turn you at my reproof: Behold, I will pour out my spirit unto you; I will make known my words unto you." The Spirit of the Lord God, the Spirit of wisdom, understanding, knowledge, and faith.

These are the promises, not because I deserve it, not because I am better than others, but because I followed the Lord and His covenants, even in the days of wars, epidemics, diseases and famines. How? Because I follow the Lord, the true God.

In the present era, it appears that the pursuit of genuine love, joy, and affluence is a universal endeavor. The quest seems to be unending, for these yearnings and are deeply rooted in the fabric of our human essence. However, what many fail to realize is that the answer to all these longings can be found in the One who created everything. He is the one who holds the keys to life itself, and He had given us the keys for free, through the Holy

Let me tell you about my Father

Bible. The only request made of us is to recognize Him and put aside our ego and intelligence, permitting Him to guide us. But before that, let me clarify one thing. No one is good except the Father, who's in Heaven. So, who are we to be claiming goodness when deep down we surely know we are all sinners? And surely you can't claim that you love your Heavenly Father while you live your life like sons and daughters of men. James 2:18 tells us, "But someone will say, 'You have faith; I have deeds.' Show me your faith without deeds, and I will show you my faith by my deeds."

Printed in the USA
CPSIA information can be obtained
at www.ICGtesting.com
CBHW051937221024
16238CB00015B/971